These are my eyes.
This is my nose.
This is my vulva.
These are my toes.

By
Dr. Lexx Brown – James, LMFT, CSE

DEDICATION

This book is dedicated to all caretakers and children in the world.
Sometimes things are hard to talk about and adults have no idea where to start. It is my hope this book helps start conversations and teaches children and their caretakers about all sorts of bodies.

ACKNOWLEDGMENTS

For Garnet & Braxton,
Hudson, Dallas, Livy, Vivy, Sophia, Jada, Mia, Zeah, Goshen, Nix, Quentin, Sebastian, Xuri, Penny, Paige, Lele, Jeremiah, Genesis, Riley, Abby, Chloe, Marcus, Maxwell and all the little people learning about themselves.

This book belongs to:

_____

_____

These are my EYES

This is my NOSE

This is my VULVA

These are my TOES

Some kids are bald and some have hair,

I have two legs, he has one,
she has no legs,
and we all have fun.

My mouth has lips, my
head has ears,

Not all kids speak,
not all kids hear

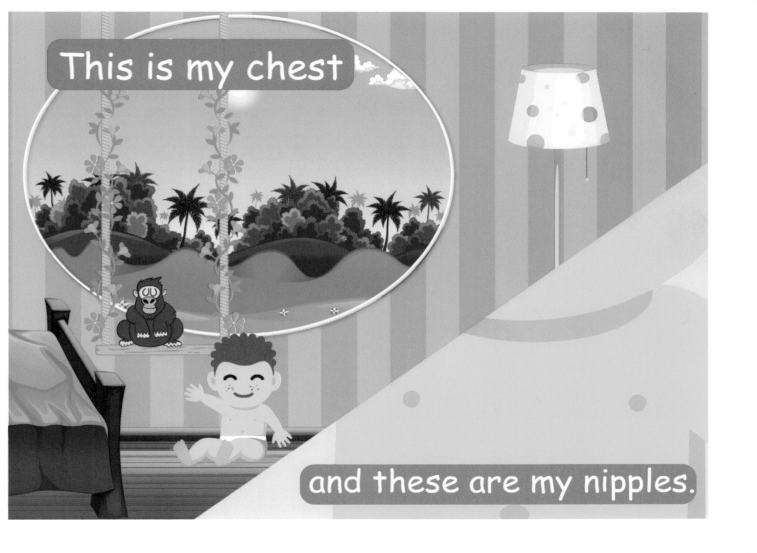

Some kids worry because they have pimples.

This is your shoulder.

This is my chin,

these are my cheeks,

and this is my throat,

where my voice sometimes squeaks

THE END

About the Author

Dr. Lexx is a licensed marriage and family therapist who works with individuals, couples, and families to help build safe, positive and healthy relationships. She is also a certified sexuality educator, who is dedicated to reducing shame, harm and stigma around sexuality topics. She resides in St. Louis, Missouri, where she operates her private practice- The Institute for Sexuality & Intimacy, LLC. The Institute's purpose is to provide accessible, comprehensive, medically accurate and culturally inclusive therapy and sexuality education for all.

On a personal note: Dr. Lexx, along with her partner, parent two daughters, who they hope to instill with body confidence and positive self-assurance.

Printed in Poland
by Amazon Fulfillment
Poland Sp. z o.o., Wrocław

64407843R00019